Hands Moving at the Speed of Falling Snow

AIDEEN HENRY

With photographs by
CARMEL CLEARY

salmonpoetry

Published in 2010 by
Salmon Poetry
Cliffs of Moher, County Clare, Ireland
Website: www.salmonpoetry.com
Email: info@salmonpoetry.com

ISBN 978-1-907056-31-4

Artwork: *From 'Passage', a collection of photographs by the artist Carmel Cleary – www.gallerycmc.ie. Reproduced with the kind permission of the artist.*
Cover design & typesetting: *Siobhán Hutson*
Printed in England by imprint*digital*.net

For Hannah, Aifric and Breffni

Acknowledgements

Acknowledgements are due to the editors of the following publications in which a number of these poems first appeared:

Crannóg, West 47, The Stony Thursday Book, Revival, The SHOp, Ropes, Southword, The Cúirt Annual, The Sunday Tribune, Ourobouros Review, Ulla's Nib, and *Wordlegs*.

Thanks to the support of fellow Galway writers in the Writers' Keep and the Galway Arts Centre Poetry Workshops.

I would like to acknowledge the cover image and images used with permission throughout the collection. They are from 'Passage', a collection of photographs by the artist Carmel Cleary. When I first saw these images, in enlarged format in the foyer of University College Hospital, Galway, I likened them to radiological images from within a closely opposed irregular joint, where the two surfaces glance off each other intimately in a convoluted dance. They are taken from Cleary's photographic tour of Utah and Arizona, where she examined the sculptural potential of the American desert landscape.

Contents

Lazy Beds

Kissing Cousins	13
Tomboy	14
Lilliput	15
Mary Ferriter	16
The fit of it	18
Undertaker	19
Tory	20
Seanchaí	21

Akimbo

Seepage	25
Not Me	26
Burren Wedding Cake	27
Bean Bheo	28
Reflections	29
Blind Date	30

Trip Switch

June 16th 2004	33
Who I am	34
Diplopia	35
Relate	36
The Ring	37
Forest Fire	38

Chordae Tendineae

Heat-Seeking Missiles   41
Unleashed   42
Penumbra   43
On the Couch   44
Deliverance   45
Hymen   46
Second Cut   47
Clawback   48

Nimbus

Hairshirt   51
Linger   52
Skins   53
Femme Fatale   54

Backspace

Single Scull   57
Over and Back   58
Drive-by   60
Pre-knowing   61
Patchwork   62
News   63
Loss   64
Shade   66

Leach

Slipstream   69
Fluoxetine (Prozac)   70
Abruption   71
Buttress   72
Trace   73
Platysma   74

Meniscus

Punching at your own weight	77
How we move	78
Induce	79
Twilight Living	80
The Place	81
Salve	82
MRI	84
Interfered With	85

Tidal Pool

Waiting Room	89
Gaelinn	90
Kerry Irish	91
Hot Yoga	92
Beginagain	93
How do they stay inside their skin?	94
Out of Touch	95
Parental Guidance (PG)	96
Coffee Shop	97

A word in your ear

Bummer	101
Poetry Class	102
The House of Forgotten Things	103
Suspicious	104
About the author	107
About the artist	107

Lazy Beds

*"The body of a starving horse cannot forget
the size it was born to."*

JANE HIRSHFIELD, *After*

Kissing Cousins

For Finbar

We gripped each other tight around the chest,
If I lift you and you lift me, we'll fly.
We were six, first cousins, and devastated
we couldn't marry.
We shared a summer holiday bed,
competed making St Brigid's crosses
and reed boats for the river,
skimming stones, jumping sand dunes,
robbing birds' nests and who could spit the furthest.
Below a white dress and short trousers,
our First Communion photos show four cut knees.

Tomboy

I want to be eight again;
my brother's stiff football boots
grip dry pavements,
as I sprint to the green,
where young trees are goalposts,
and boys forget.

When I score,
they throw their arms around me.
We are great together
until they shy away.

'She's only a girl.'

Lilliput

There are 20 men in my shower
all dressed fiercely and armed.
Does their collective subconscious
mirror their evil expressions?

Have their tiny homes been burned,
their families slain?
Are they intent upon killing
any who pass their way,
including my giant feet?

Or is it away in a soft place,
in the lap of a loved one,
dreaming of apple crumble
with feet roasting by the fire.

Mary Ferriter

RIP 1970

She had no time for Santy;
why fool the children
when life is more like eating raw rhubarb
dipped in brown sugar,
from cones of rolled newspaper.

We squelched meal through our fingers
then scattered it.
Once we helped her chase a hen,
to send it to sleep,
head under wing.

She twisted its neck,
chuckled at our alarm,
then drew us in
to the wonder of it.

As she plucked it from her lap,
a halo of feathers about her white head,
we were given one severed leg each;
pull one cord to open,
another to close,
each waxen claw.

Soon we learned to enjoy
smashing dead fishes eyes with rocks,
watching the mercury discs spill out magic,
imagining what thoughts came
from their walnut-shaped brains.

When a calf died,
she opened it
to find the plug of mucus in its lungs,
the ball of hair in it's stomach,
or nothing at all astray.

Her advice to my mother on children;
Bí ceannúil orthu,
Ach coimeád id chroí istigh é.
Be fond of them,
but keep it safe inside your heart.

She forgot they see in.

The fit of it

I study my anatomy text,
before a fire she lit,
in a room she planned,
eating cut sandwiches and cake
left out for me.
I try on this woman's family life
to feel the fit of it.
Her children sleep.

I imagine me in her wedding photos,
'I am really happy' photo,
that awkward photo with him
beside the car.
I see a young man delighted with her,
an older man uncertain,
absent to the camera.

A child wakes
I coo in her voice,
nuzzle his neck,
caress him back to abandon.
He smells of her.

Clocks tick,
the fire goes down.

Undertaker

For John Joe Conneely

I hitched a ride from Merlin Park,
surprised an empty hearse stopped.

You'll make a great corpse, he told me.
My seventeen year old innocence asked why.

Those cheekbones. Time won't touch them, he said.
I looked across at his and smiled;

Untouchable too.
We talked of college and what it might make me.

He mused at how it taught more and more
about less and less.

Tory

The island path invites me:

Stout mushrooms bark fat laughs,
squatting provocatively in the middle of a field.

Big potato rocks at the clifftop,
clamber each other's shoulders
over the edge.

Slender toadstools grace cliff walks
nonchalantly.

The burnt-orange cliff-face
scarred,
the leathery worried look
of an Afton-smoking old man.

Roundy rocks at the cliff base,
piled on each other,
like sleeping puppies.

Hillocks of grass,
miniature citadels,
flanked by granite.

Seagulls chide in low tones or
shriek panic-stricken, with oyster-catchers,
whistle-blowing football hooligans.

The sky darkens,
furious waves colonise ruthlessly;
to wash ashore seasick visitors,
who swap stories in the bar of mainland life,
deaf and blind to island teeming.

Let me be the ocean wave
that surfs ragged rock,
surge ink blue to white foam confetti,
linger after pale green,
until the next.

Seanchaí

B'annamh a chífá lasmuigh é...
It was rare to see him outside:
his bow-legged walk along the road,
a bail of hay in russet twine
slung over his shoulder,
his donkey with curled shoes
hobbling behind.

With the soft hands and voice of a philosopher,
his toothless smile welcomed us;
the whites of his eyes
against his soot-blackened face.
In the smokefilled bothán,
an open turf fire for light,
the walls were cement-grey.
Nora mooched about in the darkness.

When I stayed for tea,
it was brown bread and boiled fresh duck eggs.
Once, short of small spoons,
he shared his with me:
no question of washing.
I paused before placing it in my mouth
until I saw him wait for me to taste.

We sat for hours listening to the song
of his stories, each ending with
Sin é mo scéal.
Má tá bréag ann bíodh.
Ní mise a chum nó a cheap.
That's my story.
If there's a lie in it so be it.
I didn't create it.

When we had heard our fill,
we'd creep home, smelling of turf,
startled by the low summer sun.

In the morning 'kerry hives':
blood stains dotted our sheets.
The fleas had hitched a ride,
companion to his stories.

Akimbo

"*The fetch of a wave is the distance it travels, you said,
from where it is born at sea to where it founders to shore.*"

CIARAN CARSON, *For All We Know*

Seepage

carries a vomiting bug from sewage
to the fresh water supply,

loosens ethics
among operating obstetricians,

permeates distrust of foreigners
through a small community,

spreads divorce
through a web of friends.

Not Me

I see out through its eyes,
to its swollen bare feet.
It breathes heavily,
and listens for sounds of mice,
rustling in the attic.

It stands,
balances its front load,
then moves with a marionnette-like swing
to the window, leans forwards,
pendulous,
like a ripe tomato, heavy before picking.

Someone else's bump.
Someone else's breasts.

Burren Wedding Cake

I shelter behind a stone wall to eat my lunch.
The wind blows by like water through a sieve.
I watch a couple descend from the summit.
He careers across the plateau, clattering
uneven plates of limestone crockery.
She ambles behind.

Water burns through limestone leaving
all private layers in visible tiers.
Small stone pots remain;
some with puddles, stone holding its own
against the porous drift,
others dry, containing small stone fragments
of barren victory.

Bean Bheo (A live woman)

I recline at high tide in Galway Bay,
flick on the moon,
roll up the clouds,
wave off the sun,
rest my elbows in Clare,
my book against the Aran Islands.
My breasts swim with the seals,
while my feet jacuzzi
in the surf of the Salmon Weir.

Penguin children and seagulls scream at Blackrock;
a giant bathing is a glorious sight.

The 'Fear Marbh' (the dead man) is the name given to one of the Blasket Islands, off the coast of Dún Chaoin, Dingle peninsula, Kerry, because the shape of the island, when viewed from the mainland, looks like a giant lying still on his back.

Reflections

Apparently I will love me in you;
swear blind your uniqueness,
deliciousness, can't-bear-not-to-touchness
is the reason why, but
it is my reflection in you
that will seduce me.

Some places in me may resonate your lonesome parts;
your hands may feel found, your chin feel manly
in mine, my resolution express a forcefulness
you haven't found within,
or my softness reflect for you
parts you have not reached.
How will you feel when you see your feminine in me?
Will you trust me enough to become who you were
born to be?

Blind Date

So we will meet.

How long will it take
for the bravado to dismount,
the skin to peel back,
frailty to acknowledge itself?

Will I keep my covers on,
amuse you with my roles?
Will you tell me those things
you expect I wish to hear?

Or will we frighten each other with our rawness
then run away?

Trip Switch

*"The unconscious mind is the
true psychical reality; in its
innermost nature it is as much
unknown to us as the reality of
the external world and it is as
incompletely presented by the
data of consciousness as is the
external world by the commu-
nications of our sense organs."*

SIGMUND FREUD,
Interpretation of Dreams

June 16th 2004

Two loud bangs,
a car horn firing,
someone running,
deathly silence.
I bolt out of bed.

Out with your cousin
for a night of boyhood fun;
You have a few drinks,
steal a car,
who'll drive?

I lock in the sleeping children,
and run towards the road.
I first pass your runner,
your hat then
the car wreck.
Where are you?

In the shadow,
like a roll of disposed carpet,
you lie askew,
your limbs bent,
where there are no joints.

Your child's body warm.
Heart stopped.
Face destroyed.
Airway sealed.
I am no use to you.

You are from another world,
just two miles from mine,
where surplus children struggle.

You had no chance.
I did you no good.

Who I am

When what I do is taken away,
when what I am to those who love me is removed;
my parents love me because I am their daughter,
my children, because I am their mother,
and you, what do you see?
Who do you love?

The outer covering with its complex limited layers
housed in a female body,
or the inner essence I arrived
and will leave in, asexual, noncorporal,
revealing itself to me and you intermittantly,
through apertures of varying sizes.

This anima, with its pure voice
in unnavigated territory,
is who I am.

Diplopia

I have always been attracted by a wall eye,
the divergent squint;
That a person switches their attention between two worlds,
the seeing eye and the suppressed eye,
adopts the rules of whichever they are in
and all feels right .

The suppressed eye gazes at a whole other world,
another reality outside of this,
a country where clouds reach down their hands,
to smoothen the creases on the sea's brow,
trees uproot and pogo into the rivers, the tide is mithered
by three moons pulling on it and stones start speaking again.
These unused tracks to the visual cortex carry this signal,
like a torch shining down the labyrinth of a closed mine,
where wavelengths of light, like sound, bend around corners.

The dual reality gives depth and breadth to perception
to help accommodate whatever this life throws.
The other world in wet darkness,
a flicker lingering after the light has gone out,
a snail's track shining in its wake,
the mapped image suppressed.
Yet it is still there, even if unseen.

Relate

I ogle other people's wrists,
the flow of movement as their hands butterfly
their thoughts, fingers twirling from purple threads,
puppets in the air between us.

My ulna lies long and lonely,
its companion radius impacted and shifted away.
They no longer joke or jive together
to supinate my hand.

The surgeon will rebreak my radius,
lengthen and plate it, to house the ulna again.
There's no way of telling if the ulna will settle
or wander away from the cacophany of cartilage and bone,
to the solitude of the specimen jar
in the path lab.

The Ring

I select a soft brack
'with ring'.
They cut thick slices,
smather in butter ,
chew tentatively,
until the ring is crunched.

The victor cheers
while the two bachelors curse;
all the brack they ate
for nothing.

I wonder why my children
value the ring,
when they shuttle weekly
between parents who struggle
to be free of it.

Forest Fire

The flame dives down
through the layers of dry pine.
It smolders laterally, resurfaces at intervals
like a whale coming up for air,
then spreads underground
in circles from the centre,
like ripples from a body thrown into a canal
with no edge to limit the waves.

It holds its breath, swims further
nose forward, eyes closed,
arms by its sides;
it undulates on and on,
igniting all in its path.

Dry leaves offer themselves to it;
they become ashen spines in its wake.

Chordae
Tendineae

*Chordae tendineae are cords
that stabilise the valves in the
heart; when heart muscle contracts
the chordae tendineae tighten
to prevent the valves from
blowing backwards with
the mounting pressure.*

Heat Seeking Missiles

I send my poetry to you,
like little children
awoken in the morning,
with a kiss behind each ear,
dressed and fed while
bubbling chuckles and enthusiasms,
they dash about,
unhindered with cares.

I breathe them in
then cajole them out the door.
Did I clean their joyful faces as they chattered,
brush their lanugo-hair,
and turn them out
looking their best?

Unleashed

We lie naked on the rocks.
Sun glistens warm on drying skin.
Air,
water,
still,
clear.
Receding waves
guggle the stones.

Sensuous touch
unspools identity.
Boundaries fade.
Who is male?
Who is female?
Just covers we wear.

We return
to the grey faces,
the pavements,
time packaged again.

Penumbra

Often when you make love
your mind wanders all over:
Castlerea, Kiltimagh, Durus.

Your body routinely follows
its flock memory
to the arrivals hall.

Had you known it would be
your last time together,
you would have stretched it out for days;
dryroasted it in strips on the rocks,
salted it in parallel lines from hooks
on a tarred timber frame,
smoked it with peat and willow,
poured it with marinade
into labelled pre-warmed glass jars,
with lids to vacuum seal.

On the Couch

I find your hopes
in the nail bed of your big toe,
dreams
inside the crease of your clenched fist,
worries
under my thumbs as they splay your cheekbones,
confidences
in the soft silvery skin of your insteps.

I find your age
in your unyielding spine,
massage your ankles
while you unravel feeling,
light strokes to your naked face
as you disentangle bitter truths.
I glove your beautiful calves
with the warm pulp of my palms.
Your tears tumble.

I can only reach your peripheries.

Deliverance

Harnessed to a dying animal.
Cling.
Wait for it to tire,
bleed out,
fold to its knees,
be still.
Then ease the bindings and step clear.

Its movement pattern still burns in your memory.

Hymen

You are the river beneath my village,
a constant fresh flow,
a silent companion to my days.

I am the sea all about you,
eating into your cliffs,
tidemarking your empty beaches,
as you stare into your star-pocked sky.

Second Cut

Easier to sink in
as it cleaves the familiar path,
slices through webs of scar.

The sucking sound as steel withdraws
from soft live flesh.
Gelatinous matter swiftly gums parted layers,
obliterates the breach.
Knife, what knife? It never happened.

If only the soul had such protective instincts.
It lies with its chest bare,
trusting, gullible,
amnesic, until the sound of steel on stone reminds,
disbelief, not again,
then hurtle down the stairs of appall.

Clawback

It's over, or is it?
Your loveletter
reawakens me.

Fingers lick your-my lips,
moisten and probe.
Tongue parts gum from inner lip,
dallies with frenulum.

Rise onto elbows,
one last look,
like a wolf,
before ravaging its prey.

You-me plunge in
to the voiceless centre,
an eternal rhythm.

Hands coated with viscous gel
delve beneath the skin,
along silken muscle,

up past the cage
of the beating drum,
to slip under the skull,

where fingertips brail-read
the deep canyons, ragged forests
and serpentine ridges,
of subself.

Nimbus

*"Collect your love
and kiss the ground!"*

**Breffni's refrain,
aged 6**

Hairshirt

I can't wear enough layers;

the draft on my neck
an ice-cream face-ache,

the chill on my thigh
where your touch belongs,

the hollow in my chest
where your palms homed,
steadying the centre
of a spinning top.

Braithim uaim tú.
Cá bhfuilir?
I feel you gone from me.
Where are you?

The place you lived inside me
billows,
like a wet sheet
snapping in the wind.

Linger

Are you here?

You were,
I could swear it,
a trace left in your signature.

Your smell coated the car keys,
dripped from the metal,
as it warmed in the sunshine.

The air in the room had the feel of you,
cool, green
slightly clouded, imminent.

A piece of you stayed,
broad, explosive
in its possibilities.

Skins

The sea surface wrinkles like elephant skin
when viewed from an airplane.
Within hours of death, blood tracks to the underside,
to marble dependant skin.

Will the man who buys your shoes from the charity shop,
feel you coursing through him, while he walks?
Will his feet press out in new directions
to banish your wrinkles from the leather?

That I could bag and drop off thoughts of you,
though sometimes I click and scroll down,
relive some splendid hours and days.

Femme Fatale speaks

I am not going to get merry,
siddle up to you,
go dancing,
smooche with you,
wait to be introduced,
give meaningful looks,
long for you.

I will in the purple heather tumble you,
arms overhead
unpeel you,
chest to chest
coalesce you.
in a footbath
fingers-between-toes you.

From the grapes of me dangle you,
eyes in my fingertips
drink you,
skin on skin
envelop you,
two sweats stirred
inhale you.

I will know you,
then miss you.

Backspace

"Lie at the heart of emotion,
time has its own work to do. ...
God cannot catch us
unless we stay in the unconscious
room of our hearts."

PATRICK KAVANAGH, *Having Confessed*

Single Scull

A single scull glides the surface,
fresh water flows in the twilight,
a sunshower dimples in straight sheets.

An exercise matrix builds the stroke,
my blades grip spoonfuls in silent unison,
fluidly move in rhythm, then whoosh! on release.

Warm rain and sweat trickle down my spine,
my eyes close, balance is intuitive.
I smell the fertile vegetation.

My hands reach up into invisible pockets,
with shoulders blindly following,
my knees accordion into my chest.

My wrists snatch,
then my thighs ricochet,
and my supine body embraces.

A ghostcoach guides,
witness to the rigs of courage,
when all seems lost.

Don't look deep into the river;
there lies an irresistable call
to join the weeds.

Over and Back

Raw feelings lounge around the room:

Anger wants something done;
'Take revenge;
don't stop here.'

Sadness wants to go back to bed;
'Forget school runs, work,
turn on the blanket,
sleep for a year.'

Regret chastises me for entanglement;
without it
we could all leave now.

Dread warns 'Brace yourself;
this may hurt,
but there's always worse.'

Disbelief says 'Are you sure?
Let's hear how bad it was again.'

Hurt sits on the back of my neck,
tugging like a tethered scar.

Hollowness doubts I exist at all.

Who could eat,
and feel this bad.

Despair whispers to my heavy limbs;
'You tried everything
but it didn't work.'

Worry arranges everyone's shoes
in parallel,
laces of even length.

Nostalgia grieves her torn membrane,
spun with optimism,
crosswebbed with denial.

All regard her with a healthy dislike.

Intruders all,
unfamiliar inside the caul.
I grow accustomed.
My eyes focus on infinity.
Nothing left now but to endure.

Hands absently toss a small ball,
over and back,
over and back.

Drive-by

It comes again:
windows close,
visor down,
radio up,
wipers flap,
tears splash,
hand muffles mouth,
traffic news cautions,
too late.
Ripe grief
erupts.

Pre-knowing

Without being aware of it, some part of us registers
the feeling of a bag slipping off the back of a bike;
the sound of keys being lifted from a hall table,
before a car is stolen;
a baby's movements slowing to a halt in the womb.
A man's body expresses a despondency too,
long before his mind knows
his family is breaking up.

Patchwork

Foibles, smells, even houses can contrive
to mimic anothers, bypassing filters
to bring you directly back without warning,
still in your old clothes.

You don't know what to do there.
So you fold the covers along the crease lines,
loosen the twine, refasten the knot
where it bends in memory.
Then back on the shelf with it,
until the next ambush.

News

A sip mark on the coffee mug,
skin forms on cooling milk,
bad news hangs in stale air.
Bizarre rationale gallups.
Emotion is timelocked.
Wait 24 numb hours
for tears.

Loss

It's in the half-light, the sun eclipsed by a cloud,
which changes the color of the heather and the bog
so it doesn't look like itself anymore, but like a landscape
from a cartoon on nuclear fallout.

It's in phrases, turns of thought, odd associations
that float up when you're concentrating
on washing out cupboards, or opening a string
of knots on a child's fishing line.

It is how you feel the person beside you
in all the places they should be, but aren't;
the warm draft of their breath on the side of your neck,
in your palms as you cup their face.

It's in the half-hug a neighbour's child gives,
when they are ready to leave your lap
to face the street again. The tension returns
to your limbs once the child's dead weight lifts.

It's in the dream you have of lying curled up naked
with a man you don't have any feeling for,
but either did love once,
or are about to grow to love.

It's in that blankness, having constructed yourself
as to how you think you should look and be today,
as you walk around town,
trying to reach your feelings.

That sense of reading over your own shoulder,
outside the membrane of feeling; *What's she going to think now?*
On holidays from yourself. Like touching the underside
of your own skin, as you might reach to touch
the low damp ceiling, when swimming through a sea cave.

Loss, a palpable space, finite and concrete, sits large
in the consciousness, whether you turn from it or not.
In time, it softens and crumbles to a fine grey sand,
that blows away with passing gusts, leaving a light powdering
here and there.

Shade

All my whites drift to grey...

Yet grey is a rich deep presence, not an absence.
It is dark on light and light on dark,
a tarnished white, a paled black,
like a starched cassock or a boy's pressed blazer.
Greying hair, a temporal herald
that flags the forties, is worn as a badge
of self-acceptance or defeat.
A grey sea reflects troubled skies.

... life seen in more than black and white.

Leach

"*Poetry sings past even the
sadness that begins it.*"

GALWAY KINNELL,
Last Holy Fragrance

Slipstream

Maybe this life is conjecture.
The woman who lives in my dreams
is the real one.
She understands how she is.
The world makes sense to her.
She knows what she feels
when she looks into a coffin
or posts a love letter
addressed to no one.

Life slipstreams over her,
like cherry blossom leaves
flitting up a car windscreen,
in the April sun.

Fluoxetine (Prozac)

What will you block
or let through?
If you keep pain away, like 5HT,
I will not feel real.

You will stockpile hurt under pillows,
behind sofa cushions, for my hand to find it some night,
like my friend found her sister's earring
in her beloved's duvet.

I will view connecting memories
without emotion or care,
smirk at sorrow, snigger contempt at tears,
insentient grinning maniac.

When you fade from my neurones,
leave my thought stream,
will sadness come rushing back in
or will the programming be changed for good?

Abruption

I found death inside myself.
I had been skirting around it
not looking.

A wet patch
in the middle.

Relief.
No more wondering.

Its imprint is punched
like a logo on my retina
as I look away.

Buttress

I wonder how the bed feels
about having me all to itself.

I lie with it longer,
relieved to share
my dislocated thoughts.

When my body aches for touch,
or when worries grip,
the springs unfurl amoeboid tentacles,

the mattress curls me up,
a cheery swiss roll,
ends squirting out my creamy hair and feet.

Trace

What happens to the space
where sadness sat;
does disuse atrophy
the circuit of its thoughts?
Does some trace of the groove remain
or is it freshly ploughed with each loss?

What happens to the love
when the relationship dies;
does it transfer
to the next
or grow anew
from another source
in a different form and shape?

What happens to the role I reject;
does it move swiftly on,
to cloak someone else,
or does it hang from a nail
on the backdoor?

What happens to the habit I unlearn;
does it lie dormant,
or find another unsuspecting soul,
then taunt me from its new locus?

What happens to the insecurity I express;
does voice give it form and likelihood,
or will it cower beneath its worded shape
and slink stealthily away?

What happens to the happiness I sometimes feel;
does distrust avert my gaze,
or do I protect it
by stealing glances,
and spare it from full embrace?

Platysma

A sheet of muscle that lies
beneath the skin of my neck,
yet covers every part
of the horse's body.
So when a fly or beetle lands,
it can be flicked off
with a localised twitch.

I envy the horse
its sensored muscled mail.

Meniscus

"To paint is not to illustrate reality,
but to create images which
are a concentration of reality and a
shorthand of sensation."

FRANCIS BACON, interview 1985

Punching at your own weight

I lie in the bath,
mouth submerged,
nose above the tide.

Like Archimedes,
each breath displaces waves.

At my feet the water moves rhythmically,
a separate breathing animal.

Who would that animal be,
that inhales when I inhale,
pauses when I pause?

That silent watchful being
always accompanies me.

How We Move

The starling turns its head;
I can't see the movement, just before
and after, so I assume that it happens.
A baby watches his hands as they move
at the speed of falling snow;
he doesn't yet know they are his.
I always thought a giraffe was replayed in slow motion,
unaware that the long limbs and neck cause a temporal delay.

My insights arrive without notice;
some rapidly, cause my innards to lurch,
others in a gentle sequence,
as protective timelocks release,
like the careful unwrapping of presents.

Induce

I need a mechanical arm
with a pincer claw,
to rip out my embryo feelings
with their dangling windswept feet,
skewer them to my ear lobes,
or safety pin them to my bare chest,
where they cannot be ignored.

Twilight Living

I look to the right.
After a millisecond of inertia,
vitreous floaters skate in pursuit,
then gelatinous overshoot.

The object holds my gaze.
The floaters drift downwards.
What were they expecting?
What will hold their interest?
They are waiting for something
I don't yet know about.

Thoughts just beyond reach
echo in dreams.
Halfheard words flutter
as voices leave the room.
Blisters of rust rise
with each fresh coat of paint.

Casts cover truths,
to protect from the chaos
of really knowing.
I am on holiday from myself.

The Place

It's a schoolboy,
in a trance,
who daydreams
catching mackerel at high tide.

A lingering gaze,
upon a loved one,
in the open coffin,
before the lid is screwed down.

The full silence
at the end of mass,
released from catholic mantra,
before the crowd stirs.

The pause at the end of a car journey,
the engine quietens,
you sit in silent inertia,
before facing the house.

It's blues and greens,
bright sunlight and crisp air,
smells of grass,
and acrid otherness.

It waits for you
and has no time for duty.

Salve

I lie clenched, three inches above the sheets.
Bedclothes drape
my rigid form,
like a towel on a rail.

I try to release each part,
to lay down my weight,
but once my feet drop,
my head is up again,
a wakeful child.

Large black hands
smathered in vernix
grip the sides of my head,
spring release my skull,
ease out my swollen brain,

then reach down the back
of my neck, bowstring
my cramped muscles,
like a warm iron smoothing
damp silk.

They travel on under my skin
lengthening, quiescing
worried parts.

They turn like the tide,
leaving a settle
in their wake.

Finally soothed, my brain
fits its casing,
my limbs switch off.

The giant palms lift me
skywards, an offering
spilling over.

I dream of things
I don't yet know.

MRI

The MRI magnetises each solitary proton in the nucleus
of all the body's water molecules.
Its radiosignal causes them to flip
like compass needles. Once it ceases,
they flip back to their original orientation,
and emit a counter signal, which maps images
of the internal layers of the body.

When he left, she felt all the life drain out of her,
a constant falling from the marrow of her bones,
like the crimson flush from a lanced vein in a hot bath,
her skin became oblique, her body cells disoriented.

Interfered With

The cold draught of it,
unwitnessed.
He spoke of everyday things during.

His smell on her fingers,
like the inside of a wet anorak.
The smell stained.

She wore her hood up for months after,
hoping he would not see her,
know her.

If no one knows, then
did it ever happen?

Tidal Pool

"When the ocean surges,
don't let me just hear it.
Let it splash inside my chest!"

RUMI, *Put this Design in your Carpet*

Waiting Room

The old lady sighs, looks into space,
conflicting signals
in her forehead and eyebrows.
She did not sleep last night.

Her young companion oscillates
between attending to her
and to a bleating mobile phone,
whose texts pierce like the cry of a newborn.

She is a niece;
none of the tensions of a daughter.
Her voice shows gentle fondness,
her face hidden behind the beige mask.

Her young body tightly coiled,
leans forwards to hold the old lady's hand,
and her sacral tattoo sneaks a look out
below her jacket.

They speak of Martha who died;
that she did not fight it, that her acceptance
made her passage easier, that her best friend
had written a poem, that would make a stone cry.

Gaelinn

An Maighdean Mhara thú? a duirt sí
Cúig bliana d'aois, ag bailiu sligeáin
ar an dtráigh inniu.
Ní hea, adúrt leí.

Cén fáth nár fhoghlaim tú Gaeilge Chonamara? a dúirt sé,
É féin agus a scata leanbh, ag bailiú traenna plaisticeacha
chun oiniúin a chur.
Contráilteacht, is dócha, adúrt leis.

Kerry Irish

Are you a mermaid? said she,
five years old, collecting shells
on the beach today.
I'm not, said I.

Why didn't you learn Conamara Irish? said he,
with his scatter of children, collecting plastic trays
for planting onions.
Contrariness, I suppose, said I.

Hot Yoga

Deep breaths balloon torsos
then wring them out.

Sweat bullets shimmy,
back muscles ignite,
thighs screech,
heart pistons pound.

Knees rattle,
bare toes grip the rails
of the rubber mats.

Each colossus oscillates
below a meditating top.

Beginagain

What's there left to say,
after 40 years together,
apart from *pass the salt*,
or *has the post come yet*?

I watch an Italian couple;
She, with her Marlon Brando voice,
wall-eye, kneading gnarled hands.
He, with his thin greyness,
tobacco-paper skin, and able volleys.

Maybe sleep wipes the memory clean each night;
they have forgotten they discussed this before,
they build a house of cards afresh each day,
sure in the knowledge that they will reach agreement
on this vaguely familiar territory.

How do they stay inside their skin?

From eagles wings
the conductors hands flutter,
as though the music leads them.
Beethoven's Ninth.

Violinists perch
on the edge of their seats;
like birds on a wire
ready to alight,
expressions inscrutable as soldiers,
apart from the chief.

The drummer,
tall above the orchestra,
tames her wildness,
then lets go again.
I am sure she sprayed the graffiti outside;
'Touch not my body – Touch not my mind'

The chorus behind the orchestra,
not as I thought just VIPs
with the best seats,
roar into song.

I jump up, shake out my hair,
scale the giant trapeze,
swoop rope to rope,
strip from my body,
tadpole like Peter Pan,
out through the dome,
into a kiss.

Out of Touch

An old lady daydreams in the shoeshop,
eyes glassy with arcus senilis,

thick brown stockings in rolls at her ankles,
flesh pours over her shoes.

The assistant bellows,
she replies with raised eyebrows.

She needs his help to try on shoes
as she cannot reach her ankles.

There are islands of touch in old age:

the feel of an impatient hand
on your foot as it fits a shoe,

the clawing of the hairdresser's nails,
as she massages shampoo into your scalp,

the fruity feathery kiss of a small child,
afraid of your parchment skin,

the bone-crunching handshake at mass,
from an enthusiastic stranger,

and if you are really lucky,
the dry warm flesh of one you love
curling a stray hair behind your ear,

seeing you as you are,
inside that sagging shell,
and not as you appear.

Parental Guidance (PG)

What happens if there is a bomb in your belly,
Mommy?

Hammer-action heart
seeks exit through your ribs.
Feet under steel toecaps curl
rythmically unfurl.
Your eye is drawn
to the long dark lashes
and blue-white sclerae
of the child.
Sweat chills the back of your neck.
Taste the sour milk of fear.
Eels writhe in your bowel.
Every sound jangles.
You salivate, pant.
Muscles twitch.
Limbs itch,
anticipating
the terror and brilliance
of being blown apart,
and all you take with you.

But he's eight
so if there's a bomb in your belly,
then sadly sweetcakes,
there just won't be enough room
for chocolate crepes!

Now, homework.

Coffee Shop

Blonde tendrils corkscrew on the child's nape,
as he sits in the broad lap of his mother.
Stretch fabric defines her turgid
thighs and expands to hug her solid hips.
Her spine, rigid as a ship's mast,
her shoulders spinnaker her t-shirt
over rounded breasts and swells of stomach.

Lines flow along the curves of one,
hurtle into space, are drawn magnetically back
to land on an upward curve of the other,
centrifuge around, spin off again
at another angle, only to be lassoed back in
to another shapely landing, then crest the curve,
release and return to another parabola,
like electron satellites or the everchanging circles
of colourful chinese ribbons as they windmill
from swivelling wrists.

A Word in Your Ear

"The worst immorality is to set one's goals so low that one must crawl to meet them."

ANDREA DWORKIN,
Heartbreak

Bummer

'It is loss to which everything flows, absence in which everything flowers.'
Margaret Atwood, *The Tent*

Oh, no. Not this again.
Fucking cheerful mode.
We all know where this goes;
up blossom-strewn paths,
the world full of beauty,
engaging, trusting,
entrusting, then bam
to the side of the head,
bump down the bottom steps of reality,
overrated but true,
back to default setting,
Bummer.

Poetry Class

I don't want to sneak into your polite workshop,
sit on the edge of my seat with averted eyes,
whisper my incy mincy lines in the approved metre,
or scratch around optimistically for praise.

I'll kick out the chair from under your iambic pentameter,
rip free your expectations, fling them to the wind,
drag your emotions screaming on a wild goose chase,
then leave them for dead, as I torch the building.

The House of Forgotten Things

Tigh a' dearúid

A Virgin Mary blue and white house,
on the road west of Dingle, reminded
passers to buy what they had forgotten.

What if you could drop off what you needed to forget?
Forgotten people in the upstairs rooms,
forgotten dreams, damp on the line in the back kitchen,
forgotten promises kicking the mattresses from under the beds,
and forgotten lovemaking tossing sheets and blankets each night.

Would the store of memories and passions reach a threshold,
and self-ignited, take the roof off the house?

Suspicious

Clothes clunk to the floor
from the chair
in the middle of the night.

Did they jump
or were they pushed?

About the author

AIDEEN HENRY lives in Galway and works as a writer, physician and lecturer. Her poems have been published previously in several literary journals and magazines including *Crannóg*, *The SHOp*, *Ropes*, *The Cúirt Annual* and *Southword*, and she has given many poetry readings around the country. She was shortlisted for the 2009 Hennessy X.O. Literary Awards. This is her first collection of poetry. She also writes plays and short stories.

About the artist

Born in Waterford, CARMEL CLEARY studied photography at the Crawford College of Art & Design in Cork. Since graduating in 1990 she has received many awards and was the first photographer to win the prestigious Alice Berger Hammerschlag Travel Award, which she used for this photographic tour of Utah & Arizona in 2000. www.gallerycmc.ie